Two
Full
Circles
Undivided

Two
Full
Circles
Undivided

Poems

VOLUME 2

Wendy E. Slater

Preface

TWO FULL CIRCLES UNDIVIDED is a self-help book written as a book of transformational poetry.

What is transformational poetry?

Transformational poetry shifts how you relate to life, the questions you ask, and how you perceive life and your relation to all.

This book is for your transformation and personal growth. It is a stream of consciousness, a journal of healing, and an all-encompassing, guided journey for your mind, body, soul, and spirit.

These poems are touchstones to revisit when needed. Flip to any poem or a specific favorite poem, and you will find self-compassion, non-reactive discernment, or guidance free of judgment and obligations.

These poems and poetic healing frequencies in the writings are like water gently coursing through a dry riverbed to release stagnation or the feeling of being stuck and to bring healing and guidance wherever needed.

The poems carry wisdom for self-growth, as the words comfort, heal, and empower while quenching the soul's droughts and doubts.

This is poetry for daily affirmations and centering. It is a guide map and a beacon of light for your healing, resilience, and self-discovery.

This poetry offers a sanctuary for contemplation and mindfulness. You can open to any poem or reread the book to ground with words and poems that lead you back into your inner balance.

This poetry is a source of inspiration to guide you through any life stage.

This poetry is a wise frequency to guide, comfort, and remind you without judgment of your full authentic Self.

The poetic words flow like calm waters of solace, balm, and wisdom, soothing and releasing stagnant feelings of hurt, confusion, and grief.

This poetry was written to take you on a guided soul journey to heal, transmute, and release stagnation, wounds, and confusion and to bring clarity, support, inspiration, and comfort.

Introduction

POETRY FOR THE MIND, BODY, SPIRIT, AND SOUL

TWO FULL CIRCLES UNDIVIDED, POEMS-VOLUME 2 is a compelling book of poems. Each poem spoke to my heart and soul, and I needed to read them slowly to fully appreciate their beauty and power.

Slater's poetry immediately lifts you from the first page into your higher soul. It pulls you into the sacred fields and forgotten gardens of your true self. Its power is pure, transformative, and so very welcome. The beauty and power of each poem resonated deeply with me, as the poet's words guided me on a profound journey of the heart, mind, soul, and spirit.

To read this poetry is to sail effortlessly into a higher dimension, where the breath transforms into hand-plucking music from a lute. The only poet who has moved me so deeply is William Wordsworth. But Wendy's poetry is not ruled by iambic pentameters. Wendy's poetry dances on the page as her poetic words take root and grow with vigor and passion. This book is not just a collection of poetry. Each poem is interwoven with all the other poems, creating a profound tapestry of healing.

TWO FULL CIRCLES UNDIVIDED is a love story, a journey through the deepest forests and the wildest, most sun-dazzled oceans of the heart and soul. Thank you, Wendy E. Slater, for this book's profound healing journey. Slater, I believe, is the poet of our time.

Sheila Jeffries, Author

A BEACON OF LIGHT FOR COPING WITH CHAOS IN OUR MODERN WORLD

Now and then, a new poet comes forth with an exciting style all their own. Wendy Slater is one of those incredible writers, and this latest volume of her work continues her spirited journey of words and healing.

TWO FULL CIRCLES UNDIVIDED, POEMS-VOLUME 2 begins with a welcoming invocation for peace, after which we are blessed, once again, with the beauty of her writing. I have said before that she is a favorite amongst poets — and for me — she seems a poetry goddess who never fails to find the domains that we are all so grateful for — and longing for. I often get a sense of the great American poet Anne Sexton, embedded somewhere in Slater's attitude and in terms of a powerful influence or nodding reference that bleeds from her broken lines — a suggestion confirmed to me by Slater herself.

As usual with Slater, this book is constructed like a flowing waterfall of instinctively connected poems — all numbered and with a title basis of an 'index of first lines.' It continues from beginning to end without breaking its global structure, which revolves on a thread of closeness and distance at the same time. It is both intimate and calling in smooth or jagged observations and is a lesson in sensuality, borne on a wind of love and lust, a hunger which seems to drive it outwards and home.

If you seek a new, spiritual landscape to wander through with all its intrigues, sensuality, love, and pain, I recommend this poet to fellow voyagers. Wendy E. Slater is an amazingly unique writer, leaving on the page a refined energy—so smooth in its actions. Her style is profound and different from anything I've seen but solidly unique. Her words cascade down the page with an air of truth and personal authority. Wendy E. Slater is a first-class poet.

Peter Hague, Poet

Invocation for Peace

TOGETHER let us hold the intention that all aspects of this living planet come together in love, acceptance, and celebration of both our diversities and commonalities. Let us possess the common purpose that we heal from our hearts into compassion and forgiveness for ourselves. Together let us own the belief that we will no longer unite with blame and judgment, but come to accept that we all carry the same wounds. In acknowledging this, the hope is for the whole planet in its jubilant diversity to be healed from any and all woundings so that we come together on equal footing, living in peace and joy and setting the tone for a future of harmony within and on this planet.

Peace to all and healing to all.

For the Truth

And

The Path

To it

CONTENTS

Two
Full
Circles
Undivided

We spoke of you—

Today
She asked,
"Is he always on your mind?"

I said with grace,
"No, no, no,
He is simply in my every
    Breath."

She groaned with the
    Magnitude
        Of that.

I just
    Knew.

I water the flowers,
I tend to the garden
With roots so deep they reach into your country,
Your heart, which is the color
Pink, pink cosmos—
        My favorite.

The blooms are new,
These vigorous annuals
Not only withstand the erratic
Weather swings of Vermont,
But the flowering magenta thrives against the verdant hayfields
Which long to be cut and boxed.

In the meadow, Bobolinks search
For the tallest fescue stalks,
Swaying with the wind and singing a vivid melody
In your native tongue: love, joy, and tenderness.

These birds bring your song right into
My heart to become a symphony
With you as the conductor, creating a tapestry
Of sight, sound, and inspiration
To land in the garden of my soul.

This heart song soaks down into my roots,
Into my soil,
My summer
Sundrenched and dripping
With laughter in the
Storm.

These plants will arch and grow
With me these summer months.
Alone and fully wedded
To the beloved.

You were my galaxy,
        The planet
                I chose to orbit—
            So much more
    Than a hemisphere
        Or
            A constellation
                Pasted to the sky.

I see you now as a black hole:
        We are darkness
                Folding into
    Each other
                As the density and volume
        Of the vacuous location
                Absorbs into itself.

The equation that
    Defines our
            Collapsing event horizon is
                So complex
                Yet reveals us
    Like distilled concepts
                In a Stephen Hawking
            Book—
                Just enough of a summary
        For the general public
                To pretend to understand.

I am now leaving clues for you
  A treasure hunt
  So you may find me.

You have sung to me for years
  From the heavens
  And deep within
  The Earth.

Melodies that only you could
  Have formed
  To release me
  To release us.

I wait and know.

We are silent
　　And sit together
　Cross-legged—
Flame between
　　And amongst
　Lighting the way.

　We are stillness
　　　Together
　In the sacred heart chamber
　　　　Opening and aligning with
　　　　That star,
　　　　Your star.

You will be revealed and
　　　We will awake together.

My love for him
   Stretches to the galaxies
      Past Saturn's rings
         And into
      One constellation
         And then the next one—
   As this love has no
         Limits or defining points.

My love yawns
   And folds
      Into one light-year
         And then the next.

It's not like I'm an astronaut
   Strapped into a suit and helmet
      Propelled forth
   Looking for the outer limits
      For curiosity and definition
      And claiming.

No, it's like I'm
   Knowing and being
      Everywhere
      At once:
   A full expression without the mind.

My eyes, my cells, my RNA,
   Even my lips
      All ecstatic
      Knowing
   No boundaries
      All in the same locale
      At once:
   Love, vibrancy,

Dancing
Unowned.

The same love
    He or she
        Can feel
But this experience is from my perspective
    My angle
        Through my telescope.

Love is always love.
    The same
        Unchanging.

The longing is for you to be
    Here now
        In ecstasy of
    The day and
        Journey.

If I could be a tree
    And you were planted next to me
    As if the wind carried
    Our conifer seeds to this locale
    By destiny,
    Would our roots
    Grow down and stretch
    Deep into the
    Earth
    As well as reaching
    And branching
       Towards each other?

What would I feel or you
    When the wind brushed
    My white pine bough
    So gently or violently
       Up against you?

Would it be like a caress—
    A momentary longing filled?
    Is that why trees grow branches
    So high and long towards one and other?
    Rather, I think,
    It would
    Be; it would simply be
       One tree witnessing another.

Would I feel a void
    When the wind ripped
    The bough away
    And we could no longer touch?
    No, we would be, we would simply be
    Two trees sharing
    The space

Witnessing with vividness
  Our oneness, our lover.

Even when the wind came
  And pulled us down—
  One before the other
  We would still exist
  In love, in thought.
  The body is momentary.
    Love is always.

Would there be loss? Separation?
  No, we have always
  Been one—
  And always will be.
  We are separate and together now.
  Our hearts are the very core
  That has birthed us both.
    Two flames of the same source.

I do miss the owl that roosted
  In the core, and the thrushes
  Coming in for landings,
  The footsteps below and that dog,
  The black one, the beloved of her,
  Lovingly picking up my
    Branches for games.

Now, she is what I
  Will miss, the tenderness and joy in action.
  But she, too, is in my heart.
  Always. Lovingly always.
    Dancing, active, and alive.

Two flames of the same source.

So far our dance
      Has flung us to different
Parts and locales projected
      Up onto the freshly painted
 Kitchen ceiling
      On a dark night, starless.

We can be seen for miles and miles,
      Dancing and playing
In our different quadrants—
      As we prepare for our destiny.

I see us both. I know us both.
      Two hearts, one source.
Will you know me when you
      Hear me, my poetry?
What is the coding that will bring
      Your locale to mine?

It is there in your heart.

God, I need a man—
    Fully a man—
    To embrace and celebrate
        Life and me and us and him.
He would wear some grey hair,
    Buzzed short or even a beautiful ponytail,
    Bald and naked is okay,
        Wisdom, grace, laughter, courage,
        Brilliance, ease, culture,
        Books, tantra, Buddhism, humility,
    But full of self—the egoless kind.

    Black tie or bare-chested
    Thoughtful and reflective
  Beauty for me alone
  To see an equal—
He could touch me
    In those depths
     To unite
       Gracefully and vividly
      With the absence of ego.
He would allow
    Me to be fully hugely me
    And I him.

We will be so large, infinite actually,
    Together and so deep
        And still
    When we aren't laughing
       And staring
  I will be
  At home
       With my teacher,
     My student,
     My love,

My heart,
My flame.

Ignited and dancing
At 5:00 a.m.
As the sun crawls over the trees
Or buildings if we are in
The heart of this city or that
As we travel and roam
The planet together
An ensemble
Our music will be heard
Everywhere
With a chorus of angels
Rockin' on
As we take each step
Hand in hand.
Undivided.

One step is gospel,
The next, a symphony—Mozart,
Or a flute concerto,
And then again, the next step
Could be
Sacred chants of Tibet
Or Scottish Highland music
Or Miles, Miles Davis
Every step of the way.

I am who you think I am:
Jewish papa who denied his faith
But taught me to love Jewish deli food
And books, so many
Books.
English mama who raised me
On chocolate biscuits, shepherd's pie, roast beef suppers,
And some English rage, too.
Maybe it was the hot mustard.

And I am
A proud creative expression
Of my past
Now and hereafter
I am the one
That raised myself.

I can now raise my children.

I didn't even have the armor
    On.
I had taken 3 steps back
    From your game board
To avoid the setup:
      The archetype.
I can feel it
      And now I know it.

You have these other women
    Carry your artillery
      Aimed at me
      The ammunition is fueled
        By this utter state
          Of denial.
      This place you call home.

She was aimed
    Before I even
    Picked up the phone.
The transmission was
    One large, twisted coil.
    It made no sense
    And she pointed
Not just a finger
But attempted to trap
  Me with her stickiness.

I still have no idea what transpired.
      But she has divided us more
      And made me more certain
        Of my heritage, my knowing.

God, these people, you so
  Desperately don't want me
    To be free.

With artillery aimed
Forces mobilized
She went with your road map
Straight to the heart of
Treasure: this sacred ground
That is holy, my belly,
And you led her straight in for trespass
To the burial ground of all the worldly
And otherworldly
Treasures.

It's been the overlay of the map,
Saying, "Guilty, guilty, guilty;
Here, here, here,"
Which has actually
Honed this artillery
Exponentially increased its weight
Such that the force
Is felt like an old World War II bomb
Detonating in H_2O
With the passing of a trained Navy porpoise.

I think you've lost me
At sea. I am free.
North Star for navigation
Mermaid tail in action
Back with my whale pod.
They ironically
Anchor and ground
In this buoyant
Place beyond
Your earthly vision
And breath.

Tonight we celebrate.
Today we remove the venom

And the toxin
And heal
Ever so fully
Through the depths of ages.

I am apart from you finally.

I have quite literally fed you
   Via the umbilical cord
And you quite literally
    Starved me
      At first
    Via the umbilical cord
At second
      You quite literally
    Tainted me.

It was written quite literally
   In my code book:
"Umbilical cord remains for life"
     For feeding addicts and those who support them—
       And starving me in hopes
    That I would follow your path
Your downfall
      And be less than you
     So you could quite literally
       Feel so big
    In those small shoes.

It is as if I gave you the umbilical cord
   For you to give and take
   With opening and closing the valve
   Dependent on your world,
     Your causes, your addictions.

The tether
   Reaches deep into me
   It is mine
  But I am grown
    There is no need
   For a sour being
     To fill me with whiskey
      Or scotch drunken language
     Any longer. It's not my fault
    The ice has melted, and this drink of ages
       Is warm and no longer quenches your liver—
         But makes you stare straight into the face.

This sacredness, this right of mine
   Is separate from you
   Via the links, lines, and cords
   Now and forever.

You have betrayed
    Again and again
   With a slap or a kick
    That's so sharp and dull
  That I reel like
    I've been punched
     By a drunken man full of righteousness
     In a bar
     Or on a sidewalk in perfect view
      Of all.

I kept reaching farther
        In hope that you could touch
        My holiness and bow to our
            Divinity within together.
  The problem is for now
        Your God is denial and fear
        Mine is joy and freedom
            Ready for an explosion of ecstasy.

But the belly is where you accessed
        Me to fill me
        With your addictions
            And toxicity.

I love you and I release you
        By reclaiming and cutting
        My own umbilical cord.

I am that soft baby's bottom new
I am the virginal white
        Awaiting you in purity
I am that grey-haired woman
        Wise of energy movement
  And deep
                So deep
        Waiting
  And truly longing for true union
  So that my baby of flesh
  Can be purely and freely conceived
        And joyfully embraced
                And born
            Anew every moment.

I have sent the signal.
Are you lost at sea?
Then I'm the lighthouse
That you hear before you see.
Are you amiss in the woods?
I am the compass
The North Star that
Has always been there
To guide and orient.
Are you frightened?
I am those large loving
Hands to pull you close
To feel my heart and find courage.
Are you distracted?
I am the fresh new spring
That calls you out
Like a child
To run and play
And smell so deeply.
Are you hopeless?
I am the morning sun
Rising faithfully
Every dawn
Constant and bold
Dependably there—even if obscured.

It's early
  Sun just over the trees.
    Heavy dew
      As I walk
        The circumference
          Of the house
            Grass and cool summer
              Wetness as I re-enter
            Into the home,
            My home now.

Today I need to weed
  Plenty
    And with my hands and toes
      I will mingle with you
        As I do this
          Meditation
            Plucking and ripping

Up by the roots
  Dandelions and those others
    That I can't name
    So that the liatris,
      Anemone and lupines,
        Such gorgeous residents
        Won't be overrun.

The gifts will run freely
  In the garden
    Roaming and stretching
      And breathing
        With roots, leaves, and petals
          Dancing with their colors
          And flirting with the birds

And nested under that birch
In their garden
My belly
Which awaits
For your seed.

Oh, man!
  I am coming in for the landing
  Gently folding down
    Through the air
 To land as the bobolink
   On your stalk,
     Blade of grass.
I am ballet in action
   One pink pirouette after
   The next
And then the
   Giant leap
     Arcing across
   The floor
    Into your arms
 A leap of faith
 And you catch and
    Receive me
      Effortlessly and
    Always
 And with such
   Strength and magnitude
   And humility.

I am coming in for the landing
It's as if I took
    This running start, so many steps for an 8 year old,
    Before the take-off
And then the wild and giant
     Leap at 9, 10, 11
     Suspended for all these
       Years above the ground
     But markers below
      1, 2, 3, 4, 5, 6, 7 feet—
           Miles? Light-years?
     My God,
      This giant
               Leap and I am
    Landing at the
     Destination and grounding.

I still lock
　　All the windows and doors
　　　　Inside and out
　　At night
　　In case
　　　　　There is forced entry
　　　　　　There will be
　　　　　　Evidence, it will be known.

　　　　　It's hot, kinda blistery hot
　　　　　　For Vermont
　　　　　And those windows
　　　　　　Must be shut
　　　　　　　　Still
　　　　　　No breeze
To mingle with on the first floor—
No mention of sensuality.

　　　　　But the second story
　　　　　Is where I feel the wind,
　　　　　　Hear the owls,
　　　　　　And smell your scent
　　　　　　After the rain
　　　　　　And in bloom.

I still haven't weeded
  Instead, I skimmed
  And sifted through the pooled memories
  To strain out the slime
  And grief—really unshed tears
  Inflamed and hurt
    As a child
  And now I release
    And sieve and
  Really caress that
      Little baby girl.

Timing is divine
    Up there or in here
There must be a
    Zillion clocks
Because I have figured out
  That it's all one big yawn
  From many different angles
  Each past or parallel or future life
  In its own time frame—

Egypt—wow! That was the blink of an eye—

Pioneer woman—5-day case of the flu—

French 1920s life—three of these lives here—

The woman you sculpted as a famous artist—
    Whoa! I will be that forever.
    It's a timeless place.

We are in the car,
   My chariot,
  Very comfortable,
   We have known each other forever.

I drive, you slump.
   And we sing with the tape player,
    "Heart of Gold" by Neil Young.
    I am hollering and wailing
      It out
       Doing harmonies—
     Spontaneous and predictable joy
      Passing
        Through time and space—
      Really going nowhere
       But into
       And through
        Our hearts
       To the other place
        Called home.

I was chained down
    Into the ground
    In an unnamed dark, vacuous space.

Now I've closed the door—
    He still thinks he
    Is entitled to the key
    To my sacred
    Bodies and treasures.

My constellation was locked temporarily to his galaxy,
    Hostage in this black hole
    Poisoned by the lack of light
    Or really too much for him to handle.

I am
    Released
    And freed into the lighted rays
    Of the early dawn's birthing—
    Truly conceived in the darkest hour.

Words
    Heal.
    Words shift the
    Whole universe.

I have been drawn to arrogance
    For all my life
  As if they must have some
    Grand secret
  Deep within that vacuous space.

Frankly, all I've found
    Are empty bottles,
Gum sticking to the backs of chairs,
Mobiles from all the stolen phrases and ideas,
    Stench of semen and whiskey,
    And shoes so old and smelly that they'd
        Rot any foot that
        Had any idea
        Of sharing that space.

    There are gapless teeth and moments,
      And this weird, weird
      Exhaustion from being on
        Their tippy toes all the
        Time to get that
        Lofty look—
    The rest of us
        Should issue them
    Pink pumps or
      Stiletto heels
    Like the beginning of
    Some boot camp thing.

The thing is when you are humility
    In action
  And when you've been
      Raped again by arrogance
    Your innocence becomes
      Naiveté—

And then you stay
    Very close to
      Watch their
        Every move
          To be safe.

They become the dark black umbrella
To shield
The sun and rain
And dim your vision, hide you from view,
And you never
      Hold the handle.

I need to get him
   Out of
      My abdomen, my sacred
  Cave before you can
     Come in.
  He has this sticky molasses
     Stuff
  That he has pasted to my cave
     And now all these bats
  Are just hanging upside down in the dark—
    Guano, droppings, goo.
      What a mess.

It all reminds me of this:
     Having to apologize for every damn fight
    Scotch breath
    Cigarettes
   Seeing her so fragile
     Being so afraid
        Of her fragility
    So, I took it on again and again.
    So, the imprint was there
      Like a cigarette burnt into flesh
     But then as I got older
    It grew roots
     And branches
    And needed to be fed more.

It was alive and vivid
        So unfortunate, but true.

Love will cure all.
    This is not sticky love
  And let me feed you porridge love
    In the highchair when
      You are old enough
        To be on a
          Barstool in public view.

  This is not the love
      Of erecting speed signs
      And detour lights
      And being the
      Cop for a
      Town of 1
  Especially when we all
    Know there is no
    Cop in this town
      Anyway.

  This is not the love
      Of having the jester bring in the
        Drink at 5:00 p.m.
    To sing your song
      And be criticized and degraded
        Then soothed and smooched with whiskey breath
        Under tears—

  Love is not an action.
    It is. It simply is
    A being.
    Love is letting go of fear.

Love is tenderly bringing to The Shepherd
    A bowl of water,
    A regular occurrence,

Tiresome when you include
The lifting up and down of
Steps, the hand-feeding while
Sleeping on different floors for months.
But love
Is the feeling of her back paw
Draped over mine on the couch.
Love is speaking with her
   About death and letting
     Her know she's
     Safe and free to go.
   Love is understanding she's
A funny Shepherd—
  One with abandonment issues.
She has my support, my love
    And Windham the Wonder Dog to guide.
This is love. It is not about me.

If it is love like the Scottish Sea
   Rolling out with its secret colors,
      It will cleanse and revive
         Even if the body is
            Tired from
            Swimming alone
            So long.

My pup's here—foot dangled over mine
    Enjoying the space.
She's learned to be less claustrophobic
    Over the ages
And all these years have helped
    Healing abandonment issues
    Deep and ragged in her pelvis.

When she departs, I will not cling,
    Each tear will rejoice
        Her being, her celebration,
        Her love, and
      The knowing that
        Our love has
      Helped her—well, us—on the journey.

My life is so much freer for knowing her.

I tend to the garden
  And the water
Reaches right
  Down into your veins
Right down into the ground
  On the other side
    Of a planet
   My heart
    My belly
    My soul
   Your garden
    Albeit in your dreams
      Away from me
   I see pink cosmos
     And its roots
      And veins
     Coming right from
      My heart
     The earth
      This garden.

Naked me
  At the door
All voluptuous
  Waiting for you
I've stripped back
  Because I was
All grimy from the
    Years
Mold so thick
  And crusted
Like adobe brick
  Baking in the sun—
Time to change
  Into different
    Attire.

I am a rising star
  A planet no longer in orbit
Rather blazing and streaking
  As I arc and crest
Across the sky
  To the heart
In the constellation
    Of this space.

My light shines down
    Upon and into
You
    With grace
When you look up
    And breathe in
My momentary
    Coordinates
Dependable North Star
    Polaris
Is up
    7 fists
    To be exact.

I find you every night
    Speaking to me
Either singing or planting
    Into the earth
From this other place
    We call home.

The vulva
   Is like a ruby
   Red and so precious
   A sacred jewel.
The outer lips
   Are
  Sacred mountains
   In this world:
The holiest of sights
   The most worldly treasures—
They can never be claimed
   Or stolen
  By forced entry or
   War.
They are immutable,
   The place from which
     All the worldly quakes emerge,
   A cumulative magnitude so far
     Off the Richter scale
   A new device of measure
    Is needed.

If I were a woman
   In Bosnia,
 I would pray and say,
"My essence, my heart,
These are my country,
   My sacred soil."
The violence,
The absolute atrocity
    Can never claim
   An essence or a victory
Whether I am dead or alive,
     Chained or muted,
    Without tongue,

Breast or ripped anus, or a jagged
Knife through my heart as
I watch my husband
Die a slow death
From all the bullets, not
Random in this case.
"Why would you want this for your mother?"
I ask.

If I lived in Africa,
   —Oh, I have in my heart—
My clitoris could be apart
   From me
Hanging out to dry
         On a clothesline
   Or tossed to the rooster for
         An afternoon snack
As I probably bled, naked and ragged,
   Jagged pain from the
         Attitude, and, of course,
The instruments of the calculation
   Not just for today
      But always in this life. But not an eternity.
         "Why would you want this for your sister?"
         I ask.

The clitoris is connected to the core
Of this planet, my planet
As it reaches deep down into
Me and then you
And the earth.
The magma cultivates
And gathers force
To release all these golden treasures
So, they
Know they, too, can be in
An eternal place
Always
Knowing
Once they have
Finished weeping, wondering
And raging.
A war within.

If I wait long enough
  I will hear you
 Calling out and into
   This secret hidden place
      That attracts
 Your melody
     Like gravity's pull
 I am your moon
        That orbits
   Your home and heart
   You are my sun
        Pulling me tall
        And strong
      As my sunflower
         Petals open and peek
          And then dance
             Wildly with
          Such strength and grace.

Denmark calls to his sister
  And yet I dreamed of Africa
    With him and his brother
Hunting trophies with me.
      It was a journey of discovery
        To find my heart
      Through the savanna
        Gazelles and zebras
          Giraffes
        With heads in the stars.
            We awoke from the
              Dream
          Two hearts beating as one.

Is it me or her
    That you long for?
  Is it in your arms and heart
      Forever more
    As you gaze out
  From the docks
      Under the star,
          Her star,
        Arcing past the zenith?
        Your hands are like giant hands
              And
    You could grab
          In one swoop and pulse
          Like that star
        Before it couples into
            A constellation
    That has lock and key
    And is always
          In your heart
              Screaming.

          Why? Why? Why?

I want
　　Your hand upon my breast
　　　　Tan and ripened
　　　　From your gaze
　　　　Solidly filling me
　　　　　　　　Up
　　　　　　Up,
　　　　Up.

What do you want
　　From me?
　　Nakedness to the bone
　　Or
　　Sweet honey nectar?

I want to be tangled
　　In the rose bushes
　　With you
　Hidden from sight
　　But intoxicated
　　By the soft and
　Fresh pinkness of the petals
　　Floating down on us
　　In motion.

I want to be lying with you
　　In the hayfield
Stalks almost as tall as you
　As our backs are pressed against
　　The earth
　　And really each other
　　Under the starry
　　Black sky
　As our hands are clasped
　　To begin this
　　Wild and tender journey.

Do you want to know my life history?
　　　You know half of it
　　　Away and softly
　　　　　Apart
　I have a canvas
　　　Stretched and white
　　Waiting for the future to be painted
　　　And hung proudly
　　In my museum.
　It shall be
　　With oils
　　　Mauves and purples
　　　　In general
　　Sensual and deep
　　　As it swirls
　　　　Into my core
　　And stretches
From your one arm to the other
　　　In your embrace
　　And our joy.

I want to plant my two hands
On those luscious thick
Thighs
And
Look you straight
In the eye
As my back
Arches
Like a cat.
I want to see
The courage
And uncertainty
But definite
Love in your eyes.

It's like I've parachuted in for the landing
    Thru a dark
        Tunnel that's been
        So long
And I've landed
        Firmly and squarely
        On my feet
        Facing you.

This happened with such
    Force and intensity
        That I'm sparking
        And humming and achy
    From missing the target
            And landing
            At my destiny.

Words:

I want to be invisible
   In fact so small
  That I am that
      Star in the distant
      Galaxy that
       Shimmers into the
      Night
      So that it is missed
         And caught
         But never located.

I want to howl in agony
    At being so
        Exposed
        Truthfully
        And rawly.
  It couldn't have been
    More difficult
     To say those words to
                You.
  Were they said?
    I think the declaration was sputtered
            And stalling like
        A new driver
        With an old manual shift.

Reach in
    As I glide into 4th gear
    With your hands straddled on my hips,
        And your breath on my neck,
    Or with tanned and paint-splattered arms
        Wrapped knowingly and freely
        Along my body
            Hugging
          You and your soul.

You have known me for years.
            You trust me.
        In an instant, I love you,
          Like it's always been.

Are you ready for the explosion?
    My lord!—to be in your arms
        On your bed
          In your room
          Rocking and swaying— Wow!
     This has been simmering
       And stewing
     For years now.
   One year oregano, the next a
       Dash of wine.
     It's the meal of
     The century.
  A banquet feast
Of rose petals,
  Loose and soft,
       Amongst our tangled legs
And into those dark crevices,
    Comes our love
     To fill with joy and laughter
    And merriment
      Drunken and full
     So full
    From a simple gaze.

I have landed at this destination
    Squarely at your feet
        Solidly balanced.
    It's like you are my moon and sun
        Encompassing my heart
            Night and day.
    Your presence and love
        Is dependable and courageous
    As it has arced up and over
        Day in and out
        Obscured at times
            By clouds.
    But trust, dear one,
        And it's always there.
            I have known it
    As I know the Earth
        To be round
    Like my soft curves
        That I want
    Your hands planted on.
    There will be no eclipses
        Only comets streaking
            By
        One after the next
        Halley's, Hale-Bopp
And even little soft
            Shooting stars,
                Traceless and apparent
            As to when it all began.

I want these hands to meet your thighs
Face to face
I just want to stroke up and down
And feel those tan muscles
And really the texture
Of your leg hairs.
I watched you from afar
For years
Drinking from you
When I needed quenching
But never understanding this
Destined groove.

I want to be lying
By the fire
In your home
Of your arms
Humming and coursing
Together
As we fold into each other
After the
Meal I know
For sure you
Will prepare
And the wine
And the chilly air
Fall,
Fall,
Fall

Have courage.

I want to photograph you
And see the look
That you have for me now
Imprinted into that
Image
And to see on film
That first kiss
Passion rising
And blazing
Up from the belly
And loins
And toes
A huge wave
Of golden energy—
A heart of gold united—
And to touch your lip
With my finger
So slowly
As you suck it
Into your mouth
Feeling
It gently explore
Your inner hidden
Treasure.

I see
I feel
I touch
I taste
I hear
I know
What you want to do
In the dark
In your room
Or by the fire
Or on the docks
Under clouds or stars or moons
Or in the light at dusk or dawn
Or blazing full sun
On a boat
Or simply being in an ordinary day
As you sketch and choose
Colors
I will be plucking words
From the sky
About you
and
Love
and
Surrendering to the heart.
I smile.
I ache.

It's 3:30 a.m.
   Awake, wide-eyed, and hot.
   And I want to smear orangey-red
Lipstick all over these liquid lips
   And kiss you all over
      Your heart
   And say, "This is a heart of gold."

And then I want to apply
    Yellow like the loosestrife
      (your sister gave me)
   And say, "This is
     How to find me,"
   As I kiss your sternum
     Up and down
        And around.

Then I want pink
     Lightly on your belly
  As I am revealed
  I want the
    Colors to bring
   Rose petals soft
      And my sweet
    Fragrance
      Thru and about
   As I plant my lips
      So firmly below
       Your umbilicus—

First, the left side
   And then the right
    With a color like no other:
     Mauve almost, purple, heather,
      Cobaltish midnight blues, delicate

Passionate orange, pink orange, deep orange
Turquoise, rose—
With such depth hidden and
Only faintly revealed
Like my own.

You are all dotted and textured
Painted and loved,
Smeared and ecstatic
A map to my heart lies in this
Historic terrain of passion:
A canvas
That stretches
From one horizon to the next.
You are my Matisse.

If you could buy property right now
          In my heart
     What would it be?
First off, it would be like the Iroquois philosophy,
          You would be
          Guardian for and of the space
               For 7 generations
          Never like a fiefdom
                    Entitlement nor like a family monarchy
                         Or
               Some oligarchy in Russia.
     Simply, I would be letting you
          As a love, pink and orange,
     Into my heart, my home.

And I want to know where
          Will you be?
     Will it be some grand
          And gentle estate
     Rolling down to the water or oceans
          Waves lapping up and down
               As we make love
          On the lawn or sand?

Will it be like in London
          Hip and conservative
          With bold colors
               On the interior
               Of some elegant
          Georgian architecture?

Will it be a farmhouse
          Weathered and loved
          For an eternity?

A sandcastle that you build
      By the ocean
      Every day a different
        Creation,
    As the tides have
        Taken it in and out?

Some tropical island
      To paint me in
    Vibrant and exotic petals
      Like Gauguin?

New York? A loft
     To get lost
  In the city
    Of my heart—safely
     And vibrantly
    And with such longing that
I shudder here as I hum and sigh
    At the mere
     Thought of you.

Gummed again
    It's like my abdomen
  Is that worn leather pump
      On a hot
     Humid dripping
    August Boston
       Day
    With no shade
  For miles and miles
     No cover.

And this sole
    Has just hit
      Absentmindedly
      And
      With gravity
    A melting
      Now
     Stuck
Wad of spearmint gum
    Tossed and littered
On weathered bricks
     That have
Permitted two full
      Centuries of feet
Clad in all sorts of
    Sizes of boots,
  Sandals, leather again and again,
'60s plastic.

In my youth, my little and not so
    Little bare feet
   Blistered on the cement
    And found respite on these
  Worn, loved, tender

Bricks
That called me home
When I had
One on the bricked hill.

These sidewalks carried me up
And down
Effortlessly every day
And night
Running errands
Taking strolls
Growing and maturing
Into a city brick myself.

How sensual a memory.
Hot summer nights,
Bare feet on ancient
Worn bricks making contact
With all that life
And love
And history
Of my heart, the city.
And so, that wad
Is in this
Tenderness and joy now
Attached to my soul
Running and melting
If it could.

He is this humidity
And he has littered
The whole slope
With this goo—
I am ever so
Agile and adept
At dodging—
But she
Brought it home

On the shoe
Stucked and stayed
      For a seeming eternity
      As it plays
        Out again and again
        Ground into a groove
        As she smears this
          Garbage all
          Over the interior of my home,
                My sacredness.

It was my love for her
            That made me so vulnerable.
I was sheltered and shielded
        In ways unexpected.
I was 9 or 10 when I would
        Go to get lost
          In books, ancient cool
        Marble floors and staircases
          That could entertain any
          Kid for hours and years.
          So utterly lovely, and so cool,
          I wanted to press
  All my skin against the
  Marble on hot summer days
          And I would
  Sneak through the stacks
          Fingering and paging
          Books
            Breathing in art
          While my shoes were discarded
            Somewhere
          And those feet, my little feet,
            Felt the utter luxury
          And love of
          Being held
            By that floor
          With all that history.

Sometimes I would
Just sit
Just to feel connected
To that softness
Of the marble interior.
I always could find my dad there—
I still can
And will
And rejoice at
My forgiveness of him
And my utter wellspring
Of gratitude
For showing me how to
Root so
Deeply into earth
And the golden
Treasures of life.

What is rejection?
Fear slamming the door shut
In this case
I feel the fool
A jester
To define the other.

Today I lost a friend
        To fear,
            A loyal fear.
    I only want his hand
            As we walk
        This pink road
                Of love.
    I seem too large
            Too magnificent
        Too looming
                And dooming
        To be loved
            By him
                    Openly.

No North Star.

            I wait.

I come to the sea
  To wash away
    My grief
  And to rebuild my heart
      From placing one
    Grain upon the next
        Until I have
        The grandest
        Of castles
        To hold
        My love
      Which will remain constant
While I rebuild again and again
      And watch
      The shifting
Tides bring it in and out
        Again.

Painted pink and orange
  With love-splattered
Rays and painted
  Again and again
Not in fear or distance
But in your arms
  As you trace
    My breasts
      And
    Nipples
And dip into my
    Soul as your
Canvas
  To paint
  Love.

I make everyone uncomfortable
    When they feel
    Out of control
    I have spoken truthfully with courage.

I feel them all lined up
    To watch the parade,
        My lightness and
            Love
            Shining so brightly and innocently,
    And they gawk
At the floats
    And the grotesque
    Laid out before them
        Of me.

I have come full circle twice:
Once for forgiveness
Second to revisit
This adolescent place
Before I first touched him
And the relationship to
Cover up this terrain
Of what?

Craters, deserts, general moonscapes
Way out of touch
From my tips
Or tongue
Or toes
Depending on how one
Approaches.

This is me
Having already come
In for this lunar landing.
I have been waiting for this self-discovery
Space shuttle
For 20-plus years.

The landing equation
Miscalculated
The lack of gravity and sun
But, specifically, the orbit
Did not match
Mine.

So, I have come back in for the landing,
Perfectly off and adolescent
This time
To rescue me
And resume the healing.

There is a welcome home party in the
Shuttle
With all my friends
Timeless love:
Elka the elkhound
And Windham the pooch
Who have waited
An eternity to lick my
Face again.

This space shuttle holds
Love timeless and yawning
Of mine and for me
To bring
Me back to life,
To resuscitate
As I slip off this
Space suit,
I have been standing and watching
From the moon
For eons, so separate,
My shamanic journey,
So much more than
A simple death
Or burial alive.
I have seen it all
And I know I love you.

If I knew
  This was the next act
  Of the play,
    That you were the
      Full Circle of the
        Next volume,
    Believe me,
      My mind would have
      Halted this destiny.

I have gotten lost
        Again and again
    So that I wouldn't
      Make others
          Uncomfortable.
    I made myself
      Turn right
      When I knew
        My home and love
          Was left
      In full view
        Yawning
      And growing
          Fields of daisies, rapeseed,
            Wildflowers of every height
              And texture
    So very edible
        With you in the middle,
          A picnic spread.

            Now I have approached—landed—
              Firmly
            And you've run
              For cover
            And are so angry

For making you,
    An artist of my soul,
        Feel.

Good God,
  Just sit and be
    A man.
     Share your vulnerability.
 I don't bite
   You
 We share
   A picnic
     Of wine, grapes
     Cheese, love
       And thoughtfulness
      Precedes the passion
     An eternal wave
    Rising up between
     And amongst
    This safe land
      Of our heart
     That holds us
     Firmly in its palms
    And looks
     Deeply and longingly
      Into us
    As we are the
     Offspring
      Of the absolute:
     Love.

What is it like to have a poet love you?
        This poet?
    It's like a lion arching its head
            Back
        With a full roar
    But inside from the voice
            Comes truth and honesty
        Like a
            Newborn
                Upside down and confused
                    Slapped on the ass.
    It's like a bolt of lightning
            Coming into awaken
            From the dream
        With definition and
                Perfectly timed
        So the thunder
                Scares the hell
                Out of you
                    When it follows.
    But it's also like
            Smooth honey nectar
        Lacing itself around and
                Into you
                To heal and salve
                And rejoice
            So that we may
                Unite as
            Two full circles,
                    Two full orange circles and yellow
                Emerald green love.

It's sweetness—
    The spontaneity that rises
    Up from such depth

Will quench you
　　　For an eternity.
You will hunger no more.

But what is it like to love a poet?
　　This poet?
　It takes courage, tenderness
　　Dedication and longing
　To paint me
　Up and down
　　And charcoal to outline
Where I am and will be.
　　If you can find the courage,
　　　　Love me openly and freely.

　　Let us look
　　　　So deeply into one another
　　　　Without words
　　　As you enter my home
　　　　And touch my sacredness
　　　Such that it opens me to
　　　　Fully receive
　　　　And honor your truth.

I remain
  Whole
 Thinking of you
    Longing to run my
      Fingers over your
        Terrain of sacredness,
       Your holy altar,
        To know your unspoken truths
       Intimately and
        With joy
As they are revealed
      Deepening with our trust.
To share our bodies, solidly,
      We must be
    Honest to ourselves first.
This is not striking and resistant from the mind
        Honesty
  But a folding into the heart
      Of each other
    Honesty
      Nakedness
        Rawness
  With all its
      Scars, errors, and holdings
          Screaming, "Kiss me, kiss me, kiss me!"
          As we whisper
        You are beauty, you are wholeness,
          We are the beloved
            Birthed into the absolute
          From a springboard
            Wound way back
          For the trajectory and arc
            Across each other's
          Hearts
              Beating and propelling

Us into one another
Ecstatic joy
Vibrant truth
One beloved, two beloved
Circles united
Into one
Absolute.

I don't know if you want to
     Be a full
   Circle next to
    Mine.
  How can we unite
     Otherwise?
   Through wine and blood
      Roses and scents
       Food and texture
     Songs
  Wedded to my heart
  As I open like
   A spring blossom.

You are in my heart
        Now
You don't need to
        Shut me out
I am there
You are here
But I want
    To wrap my
      Legs around your thighs
            And sigh
          Your name
        As I let you
          Enter my sacred home
                For the first time
          I feel virginal.

It's early
    And I'm in bed
    With myself, my lover
        Which is this book
    That holds all the
        Keys, treasures
    And discoveries
      So that one day
We may find each other
    And look and
    Know
    And awaken
     From such a place
     We have
     Not touched
     Since the beginning,
Before the burp
    Of the ego,
The duality
    Grabbed or
      Clasped
    Onto this possession
      And attitude.

    I want us on
Our backs and in discovery
    With soles pressed
    Together—
    Each other's—
  As we feel
    The circuits
     Open.

This is crazy love
    Raw
    Naked
    Vibrant
    Spontaneous
    Vivid
    Absolute
On a trajectory
  A one-handed clap
  To meet your
      Heart
    That's the beginning
    Although we
     Will not
       Have truly
        Met yet
  We have
    Been dancing and swaying
      For eternity.
    I will be humming
      Like a transformer
    The vivid instant
      We meet
        Nakedly
        And
        Honestly
       Without pretense.

263

You called me onto this stage
    And now
 You are hiding
    Behind the sheer
  Curtain of ego
  With sagging and unraveling hem
  Due to your weighted stance
As you pretend no voice, your voice,
      Called me in
        As an
        Invitation
        To audition.

What is courage?
    Speaking and being
      Truthfully compassionate
        Honestly.
    Truth is not your raging
        Anger verging on hatred
      To keep love out
          Like running for
      Shelter into the basement
          From a tornado.

Open your eyes, man,
      You sent an invitation
        The play has begun
          I will keep going
      Whether or not
          You appear
        The play will
          Go on.

Some wear coats and ties
    On Sunday
  To be closer to God
      In his home
  As if he wasn't always in the heart
      When you were slouched on
          The couch
      With a flat, warm, perspiring beer
    Or screaming in your underwear
          At the children
      Or lusciously
          Eyeing the beauty
        Next to you
  Me, I am stripped back
          To be
        Closer
          To God
    One layer and then the
        Next
    Until I am
    Vividly exposed
So that when I run
  Nakedly through the fields
        The hay licks my legs
    And as I catch my breath
        Against the bark of an ash tree
      My skin says,
          "Hmmm, what am I touching
              And meeting now?"
        Divinity—
      As my toes ooze into
        The mud
    I think of meeting
        You in flesh and blood.

Two Full Circles
        United
      Into one
          Cosmic wave.
      You are my ocean,
          My beloved,
    Coming in for the
          Final meeting
              Eternal
          On the shore.
    I feel the
        Currents, the strength,
    The depths
        Out of range
        And so singularly
          A part of me
              Now.

Like a wave
     Coming in for a
   Landing on the shore,
          Your forces
      Called me
            In for days and days.

I saw you and knew
          Like gravity's pull
               Before the moment
               Arose
        As the full moon arced up
                    And anchored
          And the water
          Rose to such levels
                    Unknown before
          As the North Star
             Was and is
             Perfectly
          Polarized
             By you and us
                And what
          Could be in
      This moment
          And always.

But the water
        This course and flow had
              Been charted
              Perhaps only
              So it and you
                 Would simply
          Be of my heart
                 Always.

The wave came into
And flooded me
With such intent
And depth
Rising up through
My feet
And tailbone
Into my abdomen.

Where are you?
My honesty
Struck you
Like lightning
splitting into your heart and mind.

Now you know.

Dying lavender
  Under a full autumn moon
    Geese fly by.

Lavender stalks
  Under a full winter moon
    Snow falls quietly.

Planting lavender
  Under a full spring moon
    Rain-drenched soil.

Blooming lavender
  Under a full summer moon
    Fireflies dance with joy.

And with deep gratitude

Other poetry titles by Wendy E. Slater:

Full Circle Undivided, Poems-Volume 1

Into the Hearth, Poems-Volume 14

Of the Flame, Poems-Volume 15

The Ocher of Abundance, Poems-Volume 16

The Perspective of the Constellation, Poems-Volume 17

Visit Wendy E. Slater's website
www.wendyslater.com